The Changing Face of
Nottingham
IN OLD PHOTOGRAPHS

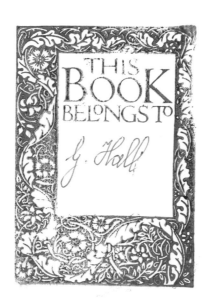

THIS
BOOK
BELONGS TO

G. Hall

Bridlesmith Gate. In 1959 the buildings on the left had not yet been demolished and replaced by new shops set further back. Through traffic was allowed and pedestrians had to keep to the pavements.

The Changing Face of

Nottingham

IN OLD PHOTOGRAPHS

Compiled by
GEOFFREY OLDFIELD

Nottinghamshire County Council
Leisure Services

ALAN SUTTON PUBLISHING LIMITED

Alan Sutton Publishing Limited
Phoenix Mill · Far Thrupp · Stroud
Gloucestershire · GL5 2BU

First published 1994 in collaboration with
Nottinghamshire County Council, Leisure
Services Department

Reprinted 1995

*Front cover illustration: Bilbie Street,
Nottingham*

British Library Cataloguing in Publication Data.
A catalogue record for this book is available from
the British Library.

ISBN 0-7509-0645-6

Typeset in 9/10 Sabon.
Typesetting and origination by
Alan Sutton Publishing Limited.
Printed in Great Britain by
WBC, Bridgend, Glamorgan.

Contents

Wheeler Gate. At first glance it might appear that little has changed. St Peter's church still dominates the scene but traffic cannot go beyond the church. Marks and Spencer has extended right up to the churchyard wall.

Introduction

The city of Nottingham today is a large one, stretching some 9 miles from north to south and 6 miles from east to west. It has grown to that size over a period of 250 years. The old borough of Nottingham, at least the built-up part, was, until 150 years ago, measured in yards rather than in miles. Its population had been growing for the previous 100 years as Nottingham's trade, first in hosiery and then lace, grew. The face of Nottingham changed, not so much because old buildings disappeared, but because new ones were built. More new buildings appeared when Nottingham was allowed to expand on the fields surrounding the town.

Nottingham changed still more in the nineteenth century when it absorbed a number of villages around the town. These too had grown during the first half of that century due to new building. The expanded town, which became a city in 1897, faced new problems as the population and trade increased, especially with the growth of traffic. The coming of the railways, public transport (at first by horse-drawn vehicles and later by electric trams and then the motor-car), lorries and omnibuses were factors which led to the changing of Nottingham, involving in many cases the disappearance of buildings and streets.

By 1920 many of the houses both in the old town and the villages added to it were old, out of date and often insanitary or overcrowded. The following twenty years saw a determined effort to rid the city of its worst dwellings which altered the existing face of Nottingham once more. A new area was created by building housing estates away from the city centre. The Second World War put a stop to all forms of building except for purposes essential to the war effort, which did not affect Nottingham's appearance a great deal. The city was more fortunate than others in England as it did not suffer much destruction from air raids. When the war ended the face of Nottingham was still much as it had been six years earlier. It started to alter again then due to the building of new housing accommodation. This took place mainly on the edge of the city, at Bilborough, where most of the new houses were pre-fabricated or built using non-traditional methods for speed of construction. In 1950 a large new housing estate was started on agricultural land at Clifton.

None of this early post-war development affected the appearance of the existing older Nottingham. Changes were to come a little later when two main factors were to alter a great deal of the city. The first of these was the need to deal with the growing problem of traffic congestion. In October 1945 the General Works and Highways Committee of the city council reported that it considered the best way to relieve the congestion in and around the Old Market Square was to build a new highway from Parliament Street near Chapel Bar and Park Row through to Castle Boulevard. This involved the demolition of property and the alteration of streets to form Maid Marian Way. This was later complemented by a further radical change of street pattern when the Broad Marsh Centre was built and The Meadows area was redeveloped.

The second feature that was to alter the face of Nottingham even more was the resumption of the demolition of older houses in various parts of the city, especially in those areas which had been added to the town in 1877. Other properties were demolished and new ones erected because of changes in the way of life in the post-1945 period. Cinemas which had been built in the 1920s and 1930s suffered from competition from television and most of them were either demolished or converted for some other use. The pattern of retail trading was another area of change, resulting in the disappearance of many shops and the building of supermarkets and shopping malls.

I acquired my first expensive camera in 1953, which cost me the equivalent of two weeks' wages. My previous cameras had the disadvantage that the photographs could only be enlarged to a limited extent. One of the uses I put my new camera to was taking photographs of scenes which I knew were shortly to disappear. The photographs in this book are a selection of those taken from about 1955 up to the 1970s. I hope that these will bring back memories to those who can remember them and that those too young to do so will realize the changes that have taken place in the face of Nottingham in the last forty years.

South Parade. The taxis now face the opposite way, most of the buildings have been rebuilt and West Bridgford no longer has its own chocolate and cream omnibuses.

Around the Old Market Square

The Council House, Processional Way and the open space either side have remained largely unchanged in the last seventy years. So too have the shops between Market Street and Queen Street, apart from the shop-fronts on the ground floor. There have been more sweeping changes on Long Row East, The Poultry, South Parade and Beastmarket Hill.

To the east, Clumber Street has been closed to through traffic, the road south from the square, Wheeler Gate, is no longer part of the main traffic artery and St Peter's Church Side has been built on.

Beastmarket Hill. Taken in 1964, this picture shows buildings which were soon to disappear, including Truman's Vaults, as well as two traffic islands.

Beastmarket Hill. A year after the previous picture, the buildings had been demolished to reveal the view of one of the new multi-storey blocks.

Exchange Walk and The Poultry. In 1974 Farmer's shop had been demolished which permitted a view of the Flying Horse Hotel on Peck Lane, before it too disappeared.

The Borough Club, King Street. The entrance to Greyhound Street can be seen to the right of the club, which moved to Market Street.

Long Row East. The late lamented Black Boy Hotel designed by Watson Fothergill, the distinguished Nottingham architect, went in 1963.

Long Row East. The vacant site on the left was soon to be occupied by Littlewoods, while further on the shop at the bottom of Pelham Street which has been rebuilt can be seen.

Clumber Street. In 1956 the well-known wine merchants and provision shop occupied the corner position with Long Row East. Then a one-way street, it is now no longer accessible to traffic.

Clumber Street. The Kardomah Cafe, at the corner of Lincoln Street, was a favourite meeting place for people to have a cup of tea and a chat. New shops were built in its place.

Clinton Street West. The shops and billiards hall over them have made way for new premises.

Thurland Street. Danks' ironmongery left us in no doubt that it was on Thurland Street.

Lincoln Street. The garage on the right being demolished in 1962 bore the name of A.R. Atkey & Co. Ltd, a business started by the man who rose from office boy in the Corporation Water Department to become lord mayor and a knight.

St Peter's Gate. The Eight Bells public house stood at the corner of Peck Lane, while Marriott's tool shop can be seen at the corner of Exchange Walk.

St Peter's Church Side. Now occupied by Marks and Spencer, this short street was, up to 1844, part of the route south before Albert Street was built to connect Wheeler Gate and Lister Gate.

St Peter's Church Walk. In 1961 the steps leading to St Peter's Gate could be approached, motorcycles permitting, from St Peter's Church Side or Church Gate.

The Making of Maid Marian Way

An attempt had been made before 1939 to keep some traffic from passing through the city centre. This was on the eastern side of the city and resulted in a continuous road from Glasshouse Street to London Road, now known as Lower Parliament Street. It was decided in 1945 to construct a similar new thoroughfare on the western side. To enable the property to be acquired for the scheme, the city council decided to apply for a local Act of Parliament. This aroused much opposition and eventually a referendum was held which rejected the proposed bill. The council had therefore to proceed more slowly by acquiring the properties needed as and when the opportunity arose.

A start was made on building what became known as Maid Marian Way, south of Friar Lane to Castle Boulevard. This involved the disappearance of Walnut Tree Lane and cutting Castle Gate and Hounds Gate in half.

Maid Marian Way. In 1962 the road was only half its eventual width and was not a dual carriageway. The Royal Children public house is on the right of the picture. The way past Castle Gate was limited because of the large factory on Hounds Gate.

Walnut Tree Lane. Part of this ancient street had already disappeared into the new road and this part led up to Castle Road.

Walnut Tree Lane. This picture shows the junction with Castle Road and the rear of the eighteenth-century houses, now housing the Costume Museum.

Castle Gate. These properties were demolished to form the western part of the new road. Walnut Tree Lane is shown on the left.

Castle Gate, looking from Castle Road. On the left-hand side beyond Newdigate House, which still remains, some two hundred year old houses were pulled down.

Castle Gate. This is another view of the houses in the previous picture.

Castle Gate. St Nicholas Rectory, designed by Watson Fothergill, stood in the path of the new road so it had to come down.

Castle Gate. Next to the Royal Children public house was St Nicholas Street which was widened by demolishing the white building on the corner to provide access to the new road.

Castle Gate and Hounds Gate. This shows properties between the two streets being demolished to make the western carriageway.

Spaniel Row. A view of the garden and rear of the eighteenth-century almshouses which were demolished although only a small space was actually needed for the new road.

Friar Lane. The vacant plot at the junction with Granby Street had been used as a surface car park since the 1930s, the attendants being supplied by the King's Roll, an organization providing ex-servicemen with jobs.

Friar Lane. This is the surface car park referred to in the previous picture with the Jubilee wing of the General Hospital in the background.

Friar Lane. The railings and gate piers of the demolished Collin's almshouses can be seen next to the Theosophical Hall, also demolished.

St James's Street. New buildings were erected on both sides of this eastern section of the street.

St James's Street. The premises at the bottom of the western section were occupied by a well-known firm of veterinary surgeons, Evered and Smythe.

Mount Street and Granby Street. As properties were acquired and demolished, the vacant sites were sometimes used for temporary buildings until the rest of the site could be cleared.

Mount Street and Granby Street. This picture, taken in 1963, four years after the previous one, shows another temporary building, the Midland Design Centre.

Mount Street and Granby Street. This shows the opposite side of Maid Marian Way, before the printing works and The Hearty Goodfellow public house were demolished. The public house was rebuilt further up Mount Street.

Park Row. All the buildings on the south side of Park Row, between Chapel Bar and Postern Street, were demolished. The properties on the north side shown here were also demolished and new ones erected.

SECTION THREE

Broad Marsh and Canal Street

When we talk of Broad Marsh we think of the shopping centre and the bus station. Originally it was the name of the street which went from Lister Gate to Drury Hill.

The Broad Marsh complex stretches from Maid Marian Way to the elevated Middle Hill and to the south as far as Canal Street. Its construction involved the disappearance of a number of existing streets and the alteration of others. A clearance scheme in the 1930s removed some of the older houses around Carrington Street.

The new development involved the destruction of one of Nottingham's quaintest streets, Drury Hill, despite much opposition which led to a public inquiry.

Canal Street. The motorcycle shop was on the corner of Carrington Street, next to the Lincoln Arms public house.

Canal Street. The fence at the side of Widdowson's machine tool works was put up after the buildings on the site were demolished in the 1930s.

Newbridge Street. This street joined Broad Marsh. The tall buildings on the left include the former St Peter's workhouse and schools.

Broad Marsh. The railway arches on the right of the picture are still there. The premises of George Lomas Ltd were one of John Player's earliest tobacco factories.

Carrington Street. The demolition of several shops provided a temporary view of the cleared site and the Lace Market.

Canal Street. The start of construction work on the complex is a scene of chaos. The rear of buildings on Low Pavement can be seen.

Drury Hill. This view from the rear shows the premises on the left-hand side going up.

Drury Hill. The buildings on both sides have been demolished but the narrow entrance from Middle Pavement can be seen on the right.

Canal Street. The site of the Crown Court formerly had a number of industrial buildings on it.

Canal Street. This shows the view of the buildings in the previous picture in 1961, taken from Carrington Street Bridge over the Nottingham Canal.

Canal Street. This view is from the same position as the previous picture after the demolition of most of the buildings.

Canal Street. In 1976 the large building on Trent Street and the railway bridge were still there.

Canal Street and Greyfriar Gate. In 1958 the weighing machine at the corner of Greyfriar Gate had been demolished and the site now has a multi-storey car park.

Greyfriar Gate. Orchard Street and Rosemary Lane, on the left of Greyfriar Gate, gave a rural flavour in name only.

Greyfriar Gate and Stanford Street. This is the view from Carrington Street after the Collin's almshouses, founded by the same family as those on Friar Lane, were demolished.

Fletcher Gate and the Lace Market

Fletcher Gate, on the west side of the Lace Market, was widened on its eastern side by the demolition of most of the buildings. The widening became necessary when the Broad Marsh centre was built and a one-way traffic system was introduced around it. The former Collin Street was extended and widened to meet the new Middle Hill, which bears no resemblance to the former alleyway with steps of that name. From Middle Pavement to Byard Lane is Weekday Cross which was widened too. From Byard Lane to Victoria Street is the street called Fletcher Gate.

The Lace Market itself has not suffered the fate of wholesale demolition due to its designation as a conservation area.

Fletcher Gate. The former chapel at the corner of Bottle Lane and the adjoining properties have been demolished recently and the site has not yet been redeveloped.

Weekday Cross and Fletcher Gate. All the buildings on the right-hand side of the picture have been demolished and the road widened.

Byard Lane. It was only a few yards from the Cross Keys public house to the Windmill Inn on Weekday Cross, at the corner of Pilcher Gate. One no longer exists, the other remains.

Warser Gate. Another public house to disappear because of road widening was the Three Tuns at the junction of Warser Gate and Fletcher Gate.

Halifax Place. These buildings were demolished as part of the widening of Pilcher Gate on its south side.

St Mary's Gate and Pilcher Gate. The demolition of the properties on this corner was followed by its use as a temporary car park. The building on the left was the Halifax Place chapel.

Hollowstone. The Horne's Castle public house formerly stood on the rocky site on Bellar Gate.

Barker Gate. This former burial ground has been tidied up and its grassy banks are a delightful sight when the crocuses are in flower.

Hockley. Some properties opposite Cranbrook Street were demolished to make way for the new Belward Street but the large mill has been converted into a public house and restaurant.

Barker Gate. These former lace warehouses were looking neglected in 1976, but have now been renovated and house offices and a restaurant.

London Road and Lower Parliament Street

Changes in Nottingham's appearance in this part of the city were brought about by increasing traffic and the drift of people away from the area. London Road was to become the main road from Trent Bridge northwards. It was of adequate width but there was a bottleneck where it joined Lower Parliament Street and Canal Street. Traffic could then turn right as well as left as Lower Parliament Street was not then a one-way street. A new circulatory road system was therefore planned with a new stretch of road between Barker Gate and Hockley, called Belward Street.

London Road. In 1962 this was still a trolley bus route and the bridge still carried trains to High Level station.

London Road. Some attempt to control traffic at this junction was provided by the roundabout in front of St Patrick's School.

Canal Street. The former police station is still there, on the left of the picture, but the adjoining properties were being demolished in 1965.

Canal Street. The barbers shop and the houses on Pemberton Street were demolished to enable the traffic to be better regulated.

St Patrick's Roman Catholic church was at the bottom of London Road which ended at Plumtree Square. The church was demolished and a new building of the same name built in The Meadows.

Lower Parliament Street. The buildings between London Road on the right and what was formerly part of Poplar Street had mostly been demolished before 1963.

Fisher Gate. All the buildings on the right-hand side have been demolished and new housing built on the site.

Fisher Gate. Some of the buildings on the opposite side from the previous picture have gone and the street is now one-way for traffic.

Lower Parliament Street. The tall house in the centre of the picture was in White Cow Yard. Its position can be judged from the Ice Stadium on the right.

Lower Parliament Street. The need for better traffic regulation can be seen in this picture taken from the bottom of Hockley in 1961. In the background is Pullman's, a drapery store founded by a man who became a mayor of Nottingham.

Lower Parliament Street. Three years later Pullman's had been demolished revealing part of Sneinton Wholesale Market and Manvers and Bentinck Courts under construction.

Pennyfoot Street. St Philip's church in 1962 can be seen in this picture taken from Manvers Street.

Pennyfoot Street. Two years later St Philip's church had gone but the former school building was still there.

Pennyfoot Street. Children of today would not have been impressed with this desolate area of asphalt and stunted grass, but it was probably the only open space for Edwardian children of the neighbourhood.

North from Upper Parliament Street

Until about 1850 the area bounded by Mansfield Road, Forest Road, Alfreton Road, Derby Road and Parliament Street was for the most part not built on. It was known as the Sand Field and was part of what was once the open fields that provided Nottingham with food. From then on for the next hundred years or so what was almost a new town grew up, by nineteenth-century standards an enlightened and planned development. Many of the houses were large ones for the wealthier employing classes. Some of them, together with shops and public buildings, have been demolished and the sites redeveloped.

Trinity Row. The row of shops and the Dog and Gun public house were demolished in 1958 and replaced by new shops with offices above.

Trinity Row. The same scene a year later, also showing part of the Mechanics Institute.

Holy Trinity church. This was demolished about the same time as the shops on Trinity Row and the name Holy Trinity given to a newly built church on Clifton Estate.

Trinity Square. By 1963 the new shops and offices on Trinity Row had been built and can be seen on the left of the picture.

Burton Street. The building on the left was formerly the home of the chief constable while to the right were the former Holy Trinity schools, then in use as the Information Bureau.

Burton Street. The same scene in 1964 shows the site being used as a temporary car park after the former school had been demolished. The site was later built on to form the Guildhall extension for the City Treasurer's Department.

Burton Street and Milton Street. The demolition of the Mechanics Institute provided a view of the police headquarters on North Church Street.

Milton Street. The buildings next to the Mechanics Institute up to Shakespeare Street and including the New Victoria cinema were also demolished.

North Church Street. Until Birkbeck House was completed the Mechanics Institute occupied temporary premises next to the Scout and Guide shop.

Burton Street and North Church Street. The cleared site of the Mechanics Institute was fenced round until rebuilding started, giving a new view of Victoria station.

Mansfield Road. The Regent Hall cinema at the corner of Peachey Street was demolished and Sandfield House built on the site. It was occupied originally by the Midland Design Centre and later by additional magistrates courts to supplement the Guildhall.

Mansfield Road. Opposite Woodborough Road was the Bluecoat School, seen behind the car showrooms. The houses on the left, on Bluecoat Street, have been demolished and replaced by new housing.

Bluecoat Street. One of the last properties to be demolished on this street was the New Church of the Swedenborgian sect.

Bilbie Street. This street, from Goldsmith Street to Shakespeare Street opposite Dryden Street, has disappeared entirely, the houses being demolished for an extension to the Nottingham and District Technical College as it was then known.

Goldsmith Street. Other buildings adjoining Bilbie Street were demolished and this picture shows the new extension under construction in 1964.

Shakespeare Street. When the college was upgraded to the status of polytechnic further expansion took place on the north side of Shakespeare Street between Dryden Street and Goldsmith Street, involving the demolition of all the properties shown on the right.

Dryden Street. From the corner of Gill Street downwards the houses on the left were demolished for the expansion of the polytechnic.

Peel Street. The demolition of the properties on Peel Street and Shakespeare Street opened up new views of the polytechnic building on Burton Street.

Hampden Street. This shows an interim stage in the demolition of the properties between Peel Street and Hampden Street.

Sherwood Street. Thomas Danks' warehouse and Nequest's music shop, near the junction with Burton Street, were demolished along with the adjoining Empire Music Hall to make way for the concert hall.

Derby Road. The Albert Hall Institute can be seen at the rear of Skills booking office but all the other buildings have gone to form the large traffic island.

Derby Road. In 1960 Chapel Bar was still a through road for traffic coming down Derby Road.

Derby Road. The Baptist church at the corner of College Street and Derby Road was demolished in about 1966 and new premises erected on the site.

Around the Victoria Centre

The modern shopping mall and bus station stand on a site which has undergone a rather different transformation from other areas of the city. In the 1890s the buildings on the site were demolished and the site excavated to a great depth for the railway station.

The building of the Great Central railway swept away most of the crowded houses and other buildings including the workhouse. As well as the station a hotel, public houses and shops were built on Milton Street and Parliament Street. Most of these were to go when the Victoria Centre was built.

Milton Street. This view from the bottom of Mansfield Road, which starts at Shakespeare Street, shows the clock tower and hotel which are still there.

Parliament Street. Between Milton Street and the entrance to the station were a hotel and shops, but the figure of a horse over the archway was a reminder that there was once a veterinary surgeon there.

Parliament Street. The boarded-up site next to the Original Dog and Partridge public house had until 1959 been an entrance to Victoria station.

Parliament Street. The buildings between the car showrooms and Milton Street had all been demolished in 1970 and rebuilding had started.

Parliament Street. The Milton's Head Hotel formerly stood on the cleared site at the corner of Milton Street.

Milton Street. This picture shows the depth of the former railway lines. Trinity Square Car Park can be seen in the background.

Union Road. The bridge over the railway line provided a view of the tunnel which took the line northwards as far as Carrington station at the end of Gregory Boulevard.

Brook Street. The building on the left housed a corporation weighing machine for vehicles but is now used as offices. The other buildings were demolished to provide a site for a new telephone exchange.

Glasshouse Street. The pedestrian crossing on the left led to a footbridge over the railway line. There is now a route through the Victoria Centre replacing it.

Huntingdon Street. This picturesque building stood in a corner of the bus station. It had been a police lodge on St Michael's playground.

St Ann's

To the east of Mansfield Road was the other common field, the Clay Field. Like the Sand Field it remained largely undeveloped until after the Inclosure Act of 1845 was passed. Most of the thousands of houses which were built were smaller than the more elaborate ones around the Arboretum, many of them in terraces off the main streets.

In 1967 the city council announced its most extensive clearance and redevelopment programme, called St Ann's, which because of its size was to be phased in eleven stages. Phase one, for which a compulsory purchase order was made in 1967, dealt with properties around Hungerhill Road. Similar orders were made for the other phases up to 1971. The rehousing of tenants and the building of new estates was a major task for over ten years, dealing as it did with the destruction and rebuilding of an area larger than some towns.

Carlton Road. Taken from King Edward Park, this photograph shows much of the eastern half of the St Ann's scheme. St Bartholomew's church on the horizon marks the ridge which was Blue Bell Hill Road.

St Ann's Well Road. The road, which took its name from a former well, provided entertainment rather different from that in earlier years. The New Victoria Hall was at one time a dance hall but became a bingo hall.

St Ann's Well Road. More entertainment was provided next door to the New Victoria Hall by the New Empress cinema which has been demolished to make a car park.

St Ann's Well Road. Stretching for nearly a mile from Bath Street to Wells Road, St Ann's Well Road divided the district into two more or less equal halves. Union Road joined it on the left of the picture.

St Ann's Well Road. The three sections of Alfred Street stretched from Woodborough Road to Gordon Road, crossing St Ann's Well Road. The central section is on the left of this picture, with the south section on the other side.

Robin Hood Chase. Until fairly recently, this tree-lined walk had some larger houses. No. 1, Locksley House, was at one time a girls' hostel.

This picture, taken from St Ann's Well Road, shows Beacon Street which sloped up towards the ridge.

Westminster Street. Many of the streets, such as this one, had terraces leading off them. The empty houses in this picture had been bricked up pending demolition to prevent unauthorized occupancy.

Pym Street. The Peveril Hotel was at the corner of Pym Street and Gordon Road. The Blue Bell Hill School can be seen higher up Pym Street.

Mowbray Street. The houses between Lamartine Street and Ferrers Street had triangular porches.

Stewart Place. Although just off the busy Alfred Street South, these houses with front gardens had an almost rural appearance. They had been erected from a prize-winning design in an architectural competition.

Alfred Street Central. The former United Methodist chapel had been used as a workshop since about 1939.

Alfred Street South and Gordon Road. Taken in 1972 this picture shows the one remaining building at the junction of the two streets, Gordon Road being the right-hand one.

Hutchinson Street. No. 8, between Northumberland Street and Alfred Street Central, had been a maltster's but was later the Nottingham Theatre club.

Cooper Street. These houses, of which there were eight, were the Bilby almshouses founded under a charity in 1709. The original almshouses were in St John's Street but were moved to Cooper Street in about 1880.

Princess Terrace. The short flight of steps led from Shelton Street to Northumberland Street.

Moore Street. Stretton Street, seen at the junction with Moore Street, had some of the more stylish houses in the area.

Bullivant Street. Between Alfred Street Central and Peas Hill Road, Bullivant Street was an example of how houses and factories existed side by side.

Hungerhill Road. Most of the houses on Broad Oak Street and Rookwood Road had been demolished to give this view. The building in the foreground was a Baptist chapel. The steep St Bartholomew's Road can be seen climbing to Blue Bell Hill Road.

Hungerhill Road. This view shows how the streets still have the original cobblestones for horse traffic.

Hungerhill Road. The last building on the left-hand side going up was a former police lodge.

Bellevue Road. All the houses had been demolished in 1971 and the retaining wall on the right was for allotments at the rear of St Bartholomew's church.

Ford Street St Mary. The corner shop had sun-blinds to stop the clothes in the window from fading.

Edgar Rise. Narrow back streets were to enable the night-soil men to empty the tub-closets.

Nelson Terrace. Front gardens were a useful adjunct for all sorts of things, such as the storage of prams and motor cycles.

Union Road. This shows one of the few larger houses in this part where terraces predominated.

Great Freeman Street. The demolition of the houses on Northumberland Street opened up a view of Alfred Street Central.

Sycamore Road. The building on the left was another lodge and the unmade track led to Hungerhill Gardens.

Alfred Street South. This factory near Blue Bell Hill Road had a house adjoining it, no doubt for the owner or manager.

Storer Street. This street off Carlton Road had six terraces like the one shown, Fairholm Terrace.

Storer Street. This former villa was used as a Salvation Army Goodwill Centre until the new one at Notintone Place was built.

Handel Street. The Vine Inn at the corner of Liverpool Street still survives.

Roden Street. The large factory at the corner of Robin Hood Street forms part of a redeveloped industrial area on the site of the demolished houses.

The Meadows

The third area of open fields to be developed in the nineteenth century was the low-lying area between the old town and the River Trent. The Nottingham Canal and the Midland Railway had already determined the boundaries on the north and east. Like St Ann's, The Meadows was built mainly with houses for the lower-paid manual workers, with workshops and factories nearby. Two important new roads were built to enable communication southwards over the River Trent, Arkwright Street and Wilford Road, with Queens Walk and Queens Drive providing a more pleasant tree-lined thoroughfare.

The year after the St Ann's scheme was started a first step towards clearing the worst of the unfit houses in The Meadows was taken. It was not, however, until the early 1970s that the face of the old Meadows began to disappear. The redevelopment of the area as housing followed a similar pattern to St Ann's, with industry being retained only on the fringes.

Arkwright Street. From Trent Bridge this busy street had shops, cinemas, public houses, a church and chapels but few houses. Muskham Street leads off in this picture to the left, while on the right Ryehill Street went to London Road.

Bunbury Street. The southern end joined the leafy Victoria Embankment but beyond Muskham Street there were terraces on both sides.

Glebe Street. The houses on Glebe Street were larger than most of the terrace houses. It connected London Road with Arkwright Street.

Colsterworth Terrace. Traffic was barred by the iron posts at one end and a wall at the other, beyond which was a similar terrace.

Arkwright Street. For a time, until Meadows Way was made, traffic northwards was diverted along Glebe Street to London Road.

Arkwright Street. Beyond St Saviour's church all the properties on both sides were demolished and the pedestrianized Arkwright Walk made as far as Kirkewhite Street.

Kirkewhite Street, stretching from London Road to Wilford Road, was divided into west and east sections. This picture is of the east part.

Cromford Street. Arkwright Street can be seen at the end of the street which was near the former Great Central railway line.

Pinders House Road. Between Waterway Street East and Crocus Street, this street took its name from what was at one time the only house in The Meadows.

Trent Bridge Footway. One of the public footpaths through The Meadows retained its right of way by a footbridge across Queen's Road to connect with this pedestrian thoroughfare.

Waterway Street East. The works building on the left of the picture still stands, but the terraces beyond have all disappeared.

Crocus Street. There are no longer any of the wild blue flowers for which The Meadows were famous, not even on the street named after them. The bridge at the end near Arkwright Street carried the railway line from Victoria station.

London Road. At the corner of Ryehill Street were the Burton's almshouses. They were demolished and new ones replacing them were erected elsewhere in The Meadows.

London Road. These larger houses extended along London Road as far as the traffic lights at the junction of County Road.

Queen's Road. This name was given to the road to the south of the Midland station in 1843 after Queen Victoria passed through The Meadows on her way to Belvoir Castle. The houses in the picture were among the earliest to be built in The Meadows.

London Road. Beyond the Nottingham Canal, just visible in the foreground of the picture, is the council's Eastcroft depot. The timber works has been demolished.

Queen's Drive. This more open thoroughfare led from the Midland station to Wilford Toll Bridge. The railway's land on the right is now occupied by houses.

Annesley Street. At the rear of, and parallel to Queen's Drive were larger houses on one side and smaller ones on the other.

Kirkewhite Street West. At the junction with Queen's Drive was the police station which has been replaced by a more modern one.

Bruce Grove. The demolition of the houses on Ryeland Crescent revealed for a short time this view of Bruce Grove. The large building is an electricity substation.

Launder Street. These picturesque houses just off Kirkewhite Street were near the recreation ground which was part of the enclosure award, as was the Arboretum in the Sand Field.

St Augustine's Street. This short street was near St George's church. The rear of houses on Wilford Road are shown.

Wilford Grove. Partial demolition has revealed the rear of properties on Kirkewhite Street.

Newthorpe Street. Between Arkwright Street and Waterway Street, Newthorpe Street had a mixture of houses and small workshops.

Newthorpe Street. These houses were at the corner of Waterway Street.

Willersley Street. At the end of the street was the elevated railway line from Victoria station to Marylebone.

SECTION TEN

Sneinton

Some of the older houses in Sneinton had been demolished under clearance schemes in the 1930s, but the outbreak of war in 1939 put a halt to further progress. After the war the housing shortage meant that further demolitions were postponed until 1950, when a compulsory purchase order was made for the Sneinton Elements area. This part of Sneinton, between Carlton Road and Windmill Lane, included the steep Prince Regent Street and Devon Street. Around one hundred houses were demolished and they must have been some of the worst examples in the city at that time, as demolition was only allowed in exceptional circumstances. The clearance campaign which was to transform the face of the city lasted twenty-five years from 1955 onwards.

Further down Carlton Road, between Walker Street and Sneinton Road, was an area where partial clearance had taken place in the 1930s. After the war the city council started to acquire sites piecemeal and eventually a small estate of mainly semi-detached houses was built. The rest of the area, including the Carlton Road and Sneinton Road frontages, was later cleared and redeveloped under more comprehensive schemes. Similar changes took place on the Manvers Street and Newark Street areas, and later on in the Colwick Road area.

Sneinton Road. St Alban's church, which still stands, is on the left and the vacant site in the centre was formerly occupied by Sneinton Palace cinema.

Sneinton Road. This shows the right-hand side looking down from the junction of Upper Eldon Street in 1962.

Sneinton Road. Keswick Street on the right had been cleared of most buildings, revealing the rear of the properties in the previous picture.

North Street. The new flats of Keswick Court were occupied in 1962 before the adjoining Salvation Army Goodwill Centre was pulled down. A new centre at Notintone Place was built later.

Notintone Place. The three houses include the birthplace of General William Booth and have been incorporated into the new Salvation Army complex as a museum.

North Street. This view looks down to Carlton Road. The Queen Adelaide public house is on the left at the corner of West Street.

Manvers Street. The buildings on the left as far as Newark Street have all been demolished including the Crystal Palace public house, one of two in Nottingham with that name.

Manvers Street. The remains of Bentinck Street and Kingston Street have given their names to the tall blocks erected on the cleared site.

Bentinck Street. From Manvers Street, Sneinton Road and the Albion Congregational church can be seen. The latter is now dwarfed by Kingston Court.

Newark Street. The timber works and other properties have all gone. The trees in Sneinton churchyard, on the right, remain.

Belvoir Hill. The formerly elegant Regency houses stood on the site which has now been landscaped in front of George Green's windmill.

Windmill Lane. The house, No. 99, has been replaced by a public house.

Windmill Lane. A photograph taken today from the same place would reveal how the face of Nottingham has changed in thirty years.

Dakeyne Street. The rear of this building can be seen in the previous picture. It was built as part of the borough lunatic asylum but later became the Oliver Hind Boys' Club.

Dakeyne Street. No. 99 Windmill Lane can be seen again in this picture.

Castle Street. The three houses on the left have been demolished and the adjoining building, formerly The Old Wrestlers public house, has been extended.

Jubilee Street. The group of houses on the right have been replaced by new ones.

Hooton Terrace. All the buildings on the left have been demolished and new ones erected in this quiet backwater of Castle Street.

Lees Hill Footway. This steep flight of steps goes down from Lees Hill Street to Sneinton Hermitage. The houses have been demolished and there is a fine view over the Trent valley now.

Trent Lane. All the houses have been demolished but the Earl Manvers public house at the corner of Colwick Road remains.

Hutton Street. New dwellings have been erected on both sides of the street. St Christopher's church on Colwick Road can be seen in the distance.

Radford

From being a small settlement near the River Leen, Radford expanded rapidly in the nineteenth century. When it came into the borough in 1877 it was the second largest place in the county, having a greater population than Newark or Mansfield. The main growth had been towards Nottingham in the triangle formed by Ilkeston Road, Alfreton Road and Radford Road, with its apex at Canning Circus. A number of smaller hamlets such as Bobbers Mill and Hyson Green also expanded to form one large urban industrial area.

When large scale clearance of unfit houses was started again after the Second World War, Radford was one of the first to be dealt with. Known as the Denman Street scheme from the road which formed the central spine, it was intended to retain some of the houses and modernize them. This idea was later dropped. Some of the industrial and commercial properties in the area were retained. More houses around Hartley Road were later acquired and demolished and another major scheme, the Hyson Green one, was started.

Derby Road. Radford met Nottingham at Canning Circus. St Helen's Street forms part of the gyratory traffic scheme, leaving the other buildings on an island.

De Ligne Street. Between Highurst Street and Canning Circus most of the old street pattern has disappeared.

Ilkeston Road. Hirst's factory at the corner of Grafton Street was one of the many lace factories which helped to make Nottingham prosperous.

Chapel Street. The gabled building of the north side was formerly Christ Church Mission Hall.

Chapel Street. By 1959 most of the houses and small shops between Chapel Street and Canning Circus had gone, leaving a view of industrial Radford.

Greek Street. One of the few streets in the area where the houses had small front gardens.

Ilkeston Road. This view from the end of Salisbury Street shows a number of streets to the right which have disappeared. On the extreme left the Ilkeston Road cinema can just be seen.

Prince Street. This is one of the side streets seen in the previous picture.

St Peter's Street. This street is named after the Radford parish church on Churchfield Lane.

St Peter's Street. These houses on Peveril Yard were formerly Radford Workhouse.

Trafalgar Street. The house on the corner of Independent Street has a curiously rounded end. Garfield Road and Warner Street can also be seen in this picture of 1977.

Norton Street. This section of Norton Street is off Hartley Road, one of a number of short streets which led to Beckenham Road and Player's Tobacco factory.

Wimbourne Road. These houses were rather better than some of the older Radford houses, which is perhaps why it was called road, not street. (Streets were usually closer to industrial areas.)

Harold Road. Despite being a road, it was very close to industry.

Radford Road. The Grand cinema, previously a theatre, was still showing films in 1956.

Radford Road. The Lumley Castle public house stood at the corner of Cornhill Street. The iron structure on the pavement was a relic from the days of trams.

Lenton Street. No. 34, despite its rather sombre appearance has a place in history having been for many years the Convent of Maternal Heart, an order of nursing sisters.

Craven Street. All the houses on both sides of the street had been demolished by 1976. On the left is St Stephen's church on Bobbers Mill Road, while straight ahead the tower blocks at Old Basford about a mile and a quarter distant can be seen.

Forest Street. The demolition of the houses revealed the rear of buildings on Radford Road with the tower of St Paul's church in the background.

Lenton

Lenton had been an important place in medieval times as the home of the wealthy Lenton Priory. Like Radford it had become an industrial village by the beginning of the nineteenth century, growing rather more slowly than its neighbour. Its acreage was five times that of Radford and when it expanded industrially it was towards Nottingham, mainly in the area around Willoughby Street. Lenton became part of the borough in 1877 and an early benefit was its connection with the town by a low-level road instead of the steep climb up Derby Road. The new road, one of the new boulevards which formed an early ring road, was at first called Lenton Boulevard but later changed to Castle Boulevard.

Lenton contained a great deal of open space stretching, as it did, as far as the River Trent with its boundary with Beeston. Some of this disappeared in the 1920s with the building of the Wollaton Park Estate and the Highfields campus and park. More recent developments have been the construction of the new road from Clifton Bridge, with industrial development on both sides and the building of the Queens Medical Centre.

Sherwin Road and Willoughby Street. The Albion Inn was on Sherwin Road which extended to Willoughby Street, beyond which is Park Road.

Derby Road and Willoughby Street. In 1962 Willoughby Street was about 550 yards long, with smaller streets to the left and right.

Willoughby Street. This view is looking north towards Derby Road, after demolition of part of the properties.

Lombard Street and Manfull Street. The short Manfull Street led from Willoughby Street to Lombard Street. Tucked away in the corner was Lenton Mission Hall.

Church Street. The eastern section led from Lenton Boulevard to Park Street. The chemists shop was at the corner of Willoughby Street and Digby Street.

Willoughby Street. This shows the existing houses on the west side near to Prospect Place in 1962.

Park Road. Park Street and Tyne Street can be seen leading off to the right. The Keans Head public house was at the corner of Tyne Street.

Gregory Street. The River Leen, from which Lenton takes its name, is here seen flowing under Claytons Bridge. The houses awaiting demolition were on Friar Street and Old Church Street.

Spring Close. In 1962 some of the houses and other properties had been demolished, while those in the picture went later. The site was needed for the Queens Medical Centre.

Abbey Street. The small building with the louvred roof is a reminder of the time when public houses brewed their own beer.

Gregory Street. The house at the corner has not had its face changed but it has had an extension at the rear. New houses have been built around the house.

SECTION THIRTEEN
Basford

The parish of Basford was a large one, stretching nearly three miles from east to west. The village of Basford was on the banks of the River Leen but by the beginning of the nineteenth century it had several smaller settlements. By 1832 there were seven villages or hamlets altogether, from Two Mile House on the west, near to what is today the Stockhill Estate, to Carrington in the south-east.

One of the fastest growing villages was New Basford which was given its name to distinguish it from the original village, which then became Old Basford. On the east side the villages on either side of the road to Mansfield gradually joined up to become Sherwood.

Most of the older houses in both Old Basford and New Basford were demolished in the 1960s. The new dwellings which were erected in Old Basford have also been demolished because of design problems and houses of a more traditional type have been built. At New Basford the cleared sites have been allocated for industry.

Church Street. Before the main road to Bulwell from Nottingham included Vernon Road, Church Street would have been a main thoroughfare. Even in the 1960s it still had a semi-rural air. Apart from the White Swan most of the properties in this picture have gone.

Church Street. A view in the opposite direction shows the old school and, on the left, how partial demolition of unfit houses left the lower walls standing if the site was not immediately redeveloped.

Church Street. On the left are the gardens of two large houses on Alpine Street. The properties opposite have all been pulled down.

Church Street. The Nottingham Co-operative Society had taken over the former Cinderhill Co-operative Society premises but it too closed as the houses around disappeared.

Lincoln Street. Beyond Nottingham Road, seen on the right of the previous picture, the street name changed. Most of the properties in the picture, including the post office in the centre, have gone.

Lincoln Street. This view of the other end of Lincoln Street was taken from the footbridge which spans the railway for those who cannot wait for the level crossing gates to open.

David Lane. This street bends to the right and then continues up to become Mill Street. All the property to the left went in the clearance scheme, but on the right there is now an attractive walk to Bulwell alongside the River Leen.

Percy Street. Several narrow streets of old houses led downhill to Lincoln Street, including Wicklow Street.

Percy Street. Further along the street was North Place, opposite the Old Basford council schools, also demolished. The trams to Ripley, written about by D.H. Lawrence, went this way.

Mill Street. There were six other public houses, apart from the Rose Inn, within 400 yards.

Queen Street. This was another of the sloping streets going down towards the River Leen. The Bulwell stone walls were probably the most valuable part of the properties.

Whitemoor Road. To the west of the main clearance area were a number of small pockets of unfit houses and vacant sites from the 1930s demolitions.

Mount Pleasant. Leading off Whitemoor Road was this street which rather belied its name.

Whitemoor Road. This house was probably of a better quality that most of its neighbours.

Basford Road. Formerly known as High Street, this road connected Church Street with Nuthall Road.

Basford Road. There were a number of terraces leading off Basford Road. Behind Breedon Cottages can be seen some of the temporary prefabs erected in 1945.

Foundry Row. Further along Nuthall Road was Cinderhill, the name no doubt deriving from the nearby colliery. Thomas North, who founded several collieries in the area, also built houses like these for the workers.

Bulwell Lane. The Midland Railway divided the village into two halves. The part to the east of the level crossing expanded, and Tinkerhouse Lane was renamed Southwark Street as far as Bulwell Lane and then became Arnold Road.

Arnold Road. The road leading off to the left is Park Lane, leading to the quaintly named Dob Park.

Arnold Road. The road junction with Park Lane has been transformed since the buildings were demolished.

Park Lane. These houses had a curious assortment of building materials in the lower courses.

Arnold Road. Just before Barlock Road (named after the typewriter company) joined Arnold Road was this house with a pantiled roof.

Mount Street, named no doubt because of its steepness. Once properties had been demolished new views were opened up. The houses on Duke Street, to the right, have all gone. The tall factory had lantern lights at the top to provide natural light.

Palm Street. The Baptist chapel and school was erected, according to the inscription over the door, in 1886.

Palm Street. Further along this street, past Wycliffe Street, was another nonconformist chapel, the United Methodist.

Duke Street. This pair of elegant houses would have been built for employers who liked to live near their work. No. 42 later became a doctor's surgery.

Mount Street. Another view of the slope from Duke Street.

Mount Street. From the bottom of the street the remaining houses on North Gate can be seen, as well as new industrial premises to the right.

Rawson Street. This illustrates how closely the people lived to industry. On the right are the Noel Street public baths.

Carrington Market Place. This district, named after Lord Carrington who owned land there, had its own small market place.

Selkirk Street. This was part of a small clearance scheme between Hucknall Road and Mansfield Road. New dwellings and shops were erected on the cleared sites.

Bulwell

When Nottingham extended its boundaries in 1877 Bulwell became part of the borough. One result of this was the construction of a new road to Nottingham. This helped the expansion of Bulwell and an area to the west of Highbury Road was developed, with houses on streets running down as far as the railway line. Shops were built on Highbury Road itself and a council school erected on Albert Street. This area has been almost completely altered since 1965, although some of the street names remain.

In 1965 the city council made compulsory purchase orders for many properties to allow for comprehensive redevelopment. These included the area between Oxford Street and Latimer Street. Other areas dealt with similarly were around Austin Street and St Albans Road. Many of the older houses north of the Market Place were also pulled down and the opportunity was taken to construct a new road pattern to relieve traffic congestion in the town centre.

Bulwell Market. Since 1970 this view has been changed by the installation of traffic lights and pelican crossings and a supermarket has been built on the site on the right.

Highbury Road. The street on the left was Oxford Street, with the Oxford Hotel on the corner.

Highbury Road. The building on the left, a supermarket in the picture, was formerly the Highbury cinema. Just beyond was Albert Street.

Oxford Street. The building on the right of the picture was part of the outbuildings at the rear of the Oxford Hotel.

Deptford Street. Like the other streets on the left-hand side of Highbury Road, Deptford Street was a cul-de-sac.

Chatham Street. This view is looking up to Highbury Road. The opening at the side of Chatham Terrace led to a footbridge over the LMS railway line.

Stone Row. This small row of houses must have been ideal for train-spotters.

Dora Terrace, at the bottom of Latimer Street. The back-yards with the outside toilets had to act as a playground for children.

Latimer Street. This view from the Highbury Road end shows a small workshop on the right-hand side.

Another view of Latimer Street taken from near the bottom.

Coventry Road. At the end of the street was Commercial Road. The building in the centre of the picture was the police station.

Coventry Road. The houses were almost opposite the Red Lion public house. The white object next to one of the doors was a boot scraper.

Newstead Street. This view from Austin Street shows the square chimney of a factory on Carey Road.

Birkland Street. This was another of the short streets which connected Austin Street with Byron Street.

Austin Street. The corner shop is at the junction of Birkland Street. At the end of Austin Street is the Newstead Abbey public house, which remains.

Chaworth Street. This was another street connecting Austin Street and Byron Street. Chaworth Street had a branch of the Nottingham Co-operative Society in the taller building on the left of the picture.

Station Road. The building on the left is the rectory which has been demolished.

Station Road. This was the main route into Bulwell from the south before Highbury Road was built.

Station Road. One can no longer cross the railway line and the station building has gone.

Spot the Difference

Can you recognize these six scenes? Although there have been changes, there are still clues in each one to identify them. Answers on page 160.

1.

2.

3.

4.

5.

6.

Answers to Spot the Difference:

1. Bath Street Rest Garden. The rest garden, a former burial ground, has not changed. The Salvation Army Memorial Hall can still be seen on the left but the Victoria Centre flats now dominate the scene.

2. East Circus Street. The hall, a former Congregational church and the buildings either side have all been demolished and the Playhouse built on the site. The tall block on the right is the ABC, formerly the Carlton, cinema at the corner of Mount Street and Chapel Bar.

3. Brewhouse Yard. The old houses which have been adapted as a museum are in the centre. The other buildings, which have been demolished, were part of the Nottingham Corporation Water Department's headquarters.

4. Weekday Cross. The former lace warehouse of Holland and Webb was demolished for road widening. The building next to it has been given a face-lift.

5. Park Row. The building on the left, at the corner of East Circus Street, remains but the rest have been demolished and new offices erected. The NCS building can be seen at the end of Park Row.

6. Canal Street. The buildings themselves have not altered but the shop names and that of the public house have. It is now The Narrow Boat.